# A Heart Full of Lavender

*Jaclyn Villavicencio*

Copyright © 2022 Jaclyn Villavicencio

All rights reserved. Independently published.

ISBN: 9798837436666

For all the people who know the darkness, but never give up on finding the light:
I see you. I am you. I love you.

This book of compiled poetry and expression is a testament to the never-ending possibility of starting over, finding new beginnings, healing, and of the beauty that your life is, can be, and will be.

*Believe it.*

Lavender, with its purple and blue hues, is known as a symbol of serenity and calm. It is a beautiful plant that brings one a sense of ease, relaxation, and most importantly, peace.

*This is a story of how I grew my garden of lavender.*

How to Grow Lavender:

Drain the Soil..................................pg. 1

Tend to the Roots............................pg. 41

Feed the Flowers.............................pg. 91

Harvest the Petals...........................pg. 133

*This is the way to healing...*

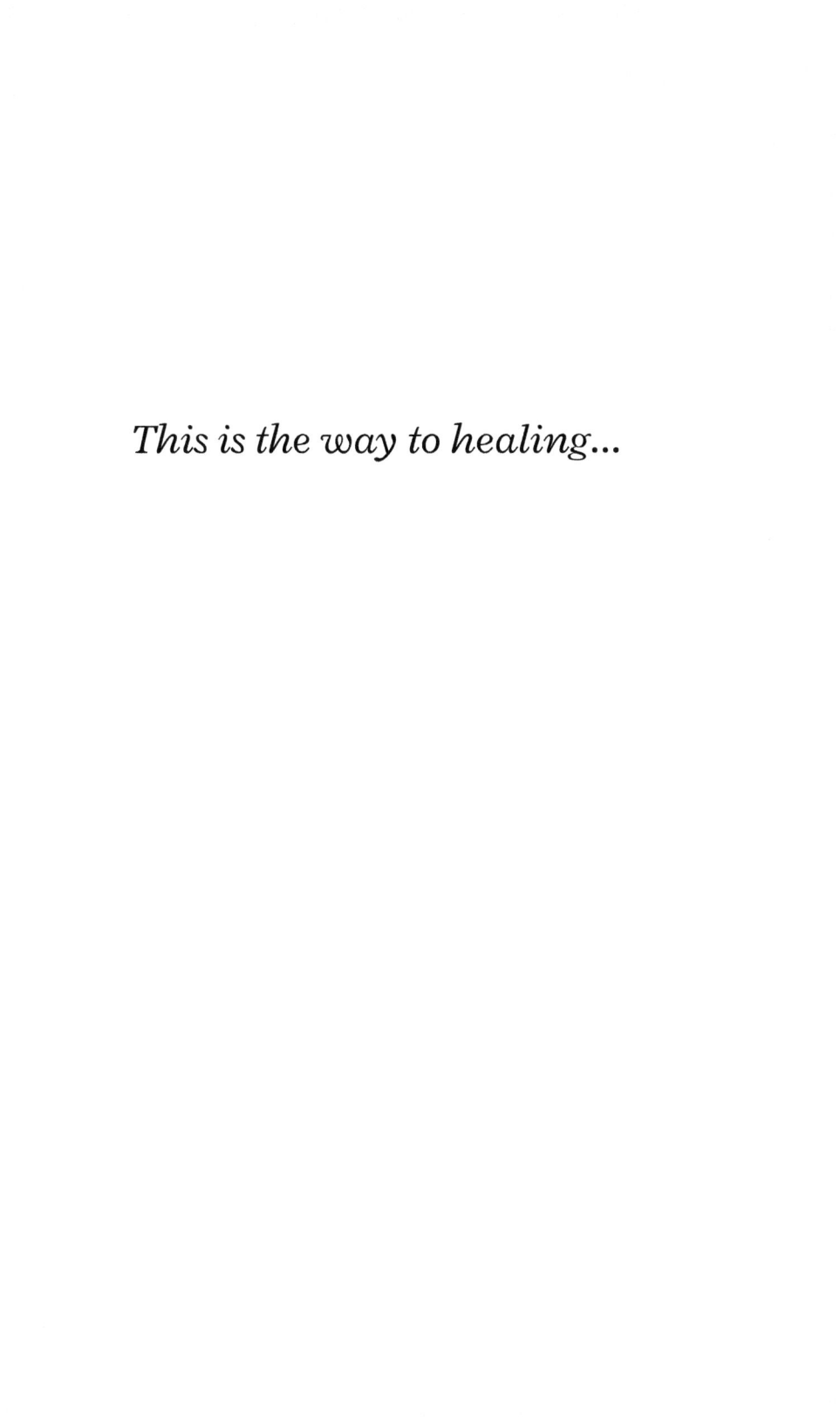

# Part I
*Drain the Soil*

*Jaclyn Villavicencio*

I used to reach for you
Eyes closed
Hoping you would reach back
And you always did
You always did,
Until you didn't
*my first broken heart*

*A Heart Full of Lavender*

She fell so hard
Like a hammer hitting a nail
She built her own coffin
Begging for his touch

*Jaclyn Villavicencio*

We could never be everything
Or nothing to each other
Like a storm building in the sky
The calm only lasts for a little while
And serves as a warning
Of the danger to come

*A Heart Full of Lavender*

I wonder how I could have given you
that satisfaction
Tricking me into smiles
That turned into tears
And later into blood

I wonder who that girl was
*I still cry for her*

*Jaclyn Villavicencio*

I can remember it like yesterday
Your dark eyes turned to black
Just like the heart in your chest

The secret you kept to yourself
For so long
Now revealed to me

*Your plan was never to love*

Shadows like you
Have never known that light

Your only capability
Was to chew me up
And spit me out

*A Heart Full of Lavender*

I've been with sick and twisted
The kind of man
Who tricks you
Manipulates you
Hits you
And makes you bleed
While you crawl back
With an apology
I've been with sick and twisted
And it won't happen again

*Jaclyn Villavicencio*

I'm not surprised I was attracted
To your storm
All my loves before
Had been small little hurricanes
The ones who keep you stuck
Scared to move from your place
So controlling you don't even know
What's good for you anymore
So when you blew onto my shore
It was a calmness
A curiosity
It was a deceit
You would end up blowing my heart in two
Breaking every piece of me
And when nothing was left to destruct
You would leave me in a pile of rubble

*A Heart Full of Lavender*

    Blood soaked panty hose
            Mascara tears
        Running from it all
                Tricked and deceived
                Confusion takes over
        Busted nose, cracked lips
             No one to save her
           Not sure the first time
       But definitely not the last time
                   *\*Neverending story*

*Jaclyn Villavicencio*

A part of me was lost the day I let him in
He took ahold of my heart
and made war with my soul
Confusing love with power
And power with violence
I didn't see it coming until his fists
Kissed my cheeks and stained them
Black and blue

*A Heart Full of Lavender*

Hotboxed the backseat
Of a Cadillac DeVille
Velvet red seats
Like the love I was dying for
Dazed, smokey clouds
I was walking into heaven
Until the doors opened back up
And I was still standing in hell

*Jaclyn Villavicencio*

I pulled you apart into little pieces
Just so my hands could put you back together

As I rolled you up into me
I licked you tight

Only to breathe you in
And feel **nothing.**

*A Heart Full of Lavender*

Those days are distant memories
    Of crowded cars
        And clouds of smoke
            Time spent laughing
        When we'd rather cry
    Running from the wolves
            Hungry for humiliation

*Jaclyn Villavicencio*

I am nothing
But the dirt on your shoes
Just like mud, I cling to you
Making it just as easy for you
To brush me off
And push me out the door

*A Heart Full of Lavender*

I didn't know what to think of her
The first time we met
Until that one time, at your place
We had the house to ourselves
A warm summer night
She was green as the grass in your backyard
She became my most familiar face
The only thing to hold me together
*The only one to numb my pain*

*Jaclyn Villavicencio*

Only so much smoke
Can numb this pain
Until it fills my lungs
And has my soul
Gasping for air

*A Heart Full of Lavender*

I want to be like flower petals
So that even when you pick me apart
I am able to grow back

*Jaclyn Villavicencio*

There is oil in the soil dear
It is poisoning the men
And making them forget how to
Love the women

There is oil in the soil dear
It is poisoning the women
And making them forget how to
Love themselves

There is oil in the soil dear
It is poisoning the children
And making them forget how to
Grow

There is oil in the soil dear
And soon, there will be nowhere
Left for us all to go

*A Heart Full of Lavender*

I can't take your hands off my neck
Your ivy vines are holding on too tight
I'm gasping for breath
As you ring me out to dry

*Jaclyn Villavicencio*

I would have danced in your fields of poppy
Because that is what love would do
But the poppy turned gray
You pushed me away
And became withered in the sun

So when the fires came
There was nothing I could do
But crawl in the flames
That took me down with you

I would have danced in your fields of poppy
But you rather sweep up my ashes
And tuck me away
For no one else to find me

*A Heart Full of Lavender*

    I've been choked out
      And spit up
         Punched and bruised
                Laughed at and humiliated
            Shattered and stitched
        And sometimes not even silently
                Sometimes blatantly
          Amid onlookers
Many who never knew what to do
              Or just accepted it
      Or didn't intervene out of fear
                And it's okay
        I get it
      I understand
What I don't understand though
      Is how we got here in the first place

*Jaclyn Villavicencio*

I just want to pour you out of me
Until every drip runs dry
Because I keep drinking from
your poisoned cup
And drowning in your flames

## A Heart Full of Lavender

I went to the fields today
To see what had grown
But all I found were broken roots
From where your hands
Had squeezed out every chance at life
From me

*Jaclyn Villavicencio*

There were days
When I saw the purest soul
It was as if love came to save the day
Curled up together
Laughing with joy
A hope growing in my heart
Of what could be
But I guess that's why
The devil is so good at what he does
He can make his favorite demons
Look like angels from above

*A Heart Full of Lavender*

They say we are all just reflections of each other
So please smile when I look at you
Smile so I can remember
I am still human

*Jaclyn Villavicencio*

You're holding on so tight
So afraid of letting go
That you've made it nearly impossible
For anything to grow

*A Heart Full of Lavender*

You don't have to pretend
I'm something you've never seen before
You look at me with borrowed eyes
That I seldom recognize
And push me down
And pull me out
Like I'm some sort of weed
A bother
A pest
And no matter how many times I try
*Still unwanted*

*Jaclyn Villavicencio*

I feel like I am in an underground tunnel again
All I can see is the darkness in front of and all around me
Flashes of light speed past
Everything keeps moving
But I am just here
Stuck standing
It is as if you chained cement blocks to my feet
But instead of drowning in water
I'm just buried six feet deep

*A Heart Full of Lavender*

I gave you the key to my garden
Thinking you would tend to all my fruit
But instead of growing roses
You nailed stakes into the ground
And turned all my love into compost
To be used for someone else
Now my garden is empty
And your sun has desiccated my soil
My land is one of many that you have run dry
And we are all still yearning for water
So our tears can finally cry

*Jaclyn Villavicencio*

He said I love you
As he gripped her neck in his hands
He said I'm sorry
As she wiped her bloody nose
He said don't leave
As he destroyed everything she owned
And she said okay
Okay because she just wanted to be loved
Okay because she was tired of feeling sorry
Okay because all she wanted was a home

*A Heart Full of Lavender*

You came to cut my roses
And only left me thorns
That I picked from my side
One by one
Leaving me with wounds so deep
All they do is bleed
And rip me wide open

*Jaclyn Villavicencio*

I knocked on death's door
more times than I can count
But your hands are weapons
That could never finish the job

*A Heart Full of Lavender*

How could the very thing
That brought you to life
be beneath you?

You should have fallen to my feet
The moment you said I love you
Instead, you took your hands
To my neck
Cutting off the very life force
that gave you breath.

*Jaclyn Villavicencio*

You watched me suffer
Like a snake in the grass
Only to tell me you also suffered
And that it was up to me to save myself
Then you slithered away
Leaving your skin on the floor
For me to feel sorry for

*A Heart Full of Lavender*

You picked me apart
Until all I had left
Were bones

For you to pour your rage on
Until it only dripped through
And turned me stone cold

The strong girl
The bold girl
The speak your mind girl
The pretty girl
The loud girl
The talkative girl
The independent girl
The joyful girl
The laughing girl
The innocent girl
**Turned into**

                                                                           The weak girl
                                                                           The bland girl
                                                                        The hushed girl
                                                                           The ugly girl
                                                                       The quiet girl
                                                                     The scared girl
                                                                        The hurt girl
                                                                   The abused girl
                                                                  The stupid girl
                                                         The black and blue girl
                                         The stitches on the face girl
                                                              ***Because of you***
                                                                         ***And now***
                                           ***She'll never be the same***

*A Heart Full of Lavender*

I'll set fire to these pages when I'm done
And rid of every word that was you

*Jaclyn Villavicencio*

You smashed dirt in my face
Thinking it would break me
With grit in my teeth
And water in my eyes
I stood
And I did
*Again and again*

*A Heart Full of Lavender*

It's true,
I found shade from your sun
In someone else's light
But not in the way you found lust
In between vines of tangled legs
I have always been the wolf
Walking in the foggy grass
As you slithered nearby waiting to strike
I have always brought bundles of lavender
To place upon your table
While you pushed bowls of pokeweed berries
At my feet
I became a sunflower after the hot summer heat
Left untouched, head hanging low
While the fox in you trotted through
Leaving your footprints deep within my soil
But as my seeds fell and kissed the Earth
I knew a new day would come
Where it was me standing tall on the mountain
While you drowned in your shallow waters
Thirsty for what you could have had
But never would
*me

*Jaclyn Villavicencio*

# Part II
*Tend to the Roots*

*Jaclyn Villavicencio*

These memories trap me
In webs of fear
That stick to my insides
And hold me prisoner
As I unclench their grip
From my mind and heart
Their sticky mess
Find new places to hide
Only to show up again
In certain places where the light touches
"BE GONE!" I say
I flail my arms as I sweep them off me
Without knowing
They still cling
To my shoulders and my back

Do you know what it is like to be betrayed by almost everyone you've ever loved?

Today,
That's how I feel
And that's the hardest part

*Jaclyn Villavicencio*

I don't want to talk about the past
But I do want to talk about how some people
Can see every ounce of you that is good
And still, rather completely break you down

They hated me for my kindness
They hated me for my advice
They hated me for my caring
They hated me for my loyalty
And they taught me
**How to keep my mouth shut**

*Jaclyn Villavicencio*

In one room
If she screamed
No one would listen
Their voices all filled up
On top of hers
In the other room
Her voice had already been drawn up
The words were already written for her
To stumble upon
And never get right

*A Heart Full of Lavender*

I can't find the sun
Sometimes I don't want to
Sometimes I want to sit in the pain, in the tears,
in the hurt
If that is all that I have left of you
*I'll take it*

*Jaclyn Villavicencio*

This is me cleaning out your closet
                This is me setting your guilt free
      This is me finding forgiveness
                      Except I still can't
                            **Breathe**

*A Heart Full of Lavender*

I guess I'm the fool
For making you believe
I was okay for all these years
For a while there
I thought I was okay, too
But now I am feeling
The grips of this cage
Around my lungs
More and more
Each day
I can't breathe
I can't feel the air
And if you're not careful
You may just
Suffocate me

*Jaclyn Villavicencio*

I'm tired of climbing
The hills have become too high
And I keep scraping my knees
Just trying to hold on
Help me up
Take my hand
Give me something to believe in again

*A Heart Full of Lavender*

I trace fingers along the path of old memories
That only lead to pain and humiliation
They are cracks in the sidewalk that trip me
And as I stumble
I discover why I keep walking away
From every person who seems real

*Jaclyn Villavicencio*

You walked in...
*I was triggered*

*A Heart Full of Lavender*

Sometimes we find ourselves
Revisiting the dark spots of our past
The places that sneak up on us in a daydream
And cause chaos to our souls
These are the places we hide
This is our trauma
And it returns every so often
Begging to be healed

*Jaclyn Villavicencio*

It still comes up sometimes
When the tequila gets to talking
She told me to get over it
And I have
But this pain doesn't seem to have
An expiration date

*A Heart Full of Lavender*

I'm still broken it seems
Cracking at my seams
And I don't know how
To pull me back together

I'm still broken it seems
Cracking at my seams
And I can't look in my own eyes
Because it makes me want to scream

I'm still broken it seems
Cracking at my seams
And I'm scared I will break
Beyond repair

I'm still broken it seems
Cracking at my seams
How do I get out of here
Someone help me out of here

*Jaclyn Villavicencio*

Pain has no time limit
Whoever told you that
**Is a liar.**

If I let it go
Does it mean you defeated me?
I guess I have always been loyal to the cause
But I am not the one to serve your justice
Because forgiving you doesn't free you
    *But it is what will give me wings*

*Jaclyn Villavicencio*

Why do we have to break to be free?
Why does our hurt have to ache
for us to find peace?

*A Heart Full of Lavender*

Are you going to wash me away?
Bring me peace again
Comfort me with your waters
And heal what's left within
The tide moves in
The tide moves out
My heart beats just the same
So please drench my soul
And erase my pain

*Jaclyn Villavicencio*

The intense beating of my heart
It's happening again
The rush of panic
My thoughts unclear
Like an upside-down map
I can't find my way out of here

*A Heart Full of Lavender*

I don't want to hold onto this anymore
My hurt has been sprinkled in my cells
And bursts when least expected
I don't want to hold onto this anymore
But how do you let go of something
from a lifetime ago
How do you release
a past you no longer recognize
But still creeps up on you

*Jaclyn Villavicencio*

I wish I knew about forgiveness
So I could forgive you
So I could forgive myself
We've spent so much time in the turbulence
It is so hard to remember
How to fly

*A Heart Full of Lavender*

You hurt me
We both know it is true
It is probably true that somewhere
Maybe I hurt you too
But what hurts the most
Is holding on to it all
I rather just let it go
Even if that means forgiving you

*Jaclyn Villavicencio*

My hands tremble
    My stomach sinks
        And it is so hard to stop
            Replaying your nightmare

*A Heart Full of Lavender*

If only I could be soft and sweet
But it seems every time I open my mouth
to speak
It only sprays bullets

*Jaclyn Villavicencio*

My coldness stops you in your tracks
Like a sharp piece of fallen ice
I can't help myself sometimes
I scream before I think
I worry before I live
And it all becomes an endless cycle
Of heated words
My poor heart works as a weapon
So it is never hurt again

*A Heart Full of Lavender*

Some days I feel proud for surviving you
On other days I still feel like a victim
Broken on the floor
Crying in my hands
Screaming up to the stars
That do not shine for me anymore

*Jaclyn Villavicencio*

Sometimes I want to cry
I can feel the tears building up
But then
Nothing falls
Am I as dry and cold
As I'm beginning to believe?

That tension in your chest that you are feeling - that is you not living your truth. That is you still saying yes to the things that do not serve you. That is you not speaking the things you want to say. That feeling will continue to grow and grow to remind you that if you keep turning from your truth - *it will break you wide open.*

*Jaclyn Villavicencio*

How do you forgive someone
that has caused so much pain?
How do you say that it is okay
for what you did to me?

*A Heart Full of Lavender*

We knew so much about each other's past
The dark lows of desperation
The evil that leached into our hearts

We made it out alive
Only for one of us to betray the other
A heartache never to be forgotten

*You can take the knife*
*Out of my back now*

*Jaclyn Villavicencio*

If I am being honest
I always felt different
Like I never fit
A puzzle piece
Put in the wrong box

*A Heart Full of Lavender*

It is hard to be yourself
When everywhere you've turned
And everywhere you've looked
You've been told not to
It's hard to be yourself
When you don't know
Who **you** is

*Jaclyn Villavicencio*

It is like the winter has come
And covered frost upon my soul
Tightening its freezing grip
Around my roots

I'm so lost in the cold
Finding forgiveness
May have to wait
Until spring

*A Heart Full of Lavender*

One day when the dust settles
And all my pain is lying on the floor
Maybe then you will have what it takes
To pick me up
*And help stitch me back together*

*Jaclyn Villavicencio*

Just when I think it is over
My shell cracks
Revealing all the scars left behind
You, me, and paranoia
What a horrible memory
But one that will not be my legacy
And that's why I write this down
My words may seem dark to some
But to others...
They are just the breath they need
To start over

Sometimes to heal, you have to go back. You have to retrace your steps. You have to step back into those moments and really feel your story. You do this not so you can stuff those feelings back down. You do this to give those feelings wings. Wings to fly free. You go back, so you can finally let go.

*Jaclyn Villavicencio*

My brain is filled with morning glory
I can't seem to clear it out
Or keep it from growing

But it's hard
To find me
In there

It is like I can't breathe
There is so much pressure on my chest
I'm like a balloon
But instead of floating
I am about to pop wide open
And fall to pieces everywhere

*Jaclyn Villavicencio*

I can't come today
Because I am so lost in my mind
I am finding it hard to find
The road home
These thoughts of gravel feel sharp
Beneath my feet
And this dark sky of thoughts
Is hiding any inch of light that might be left

May my breath be a beacon
A sound of safety
As I navigate through this fear
And search for my home
Deep within my heart

*A Heart Full of Lavender*

Half of me is at peace
Half of me is at war
Is this what they mean when they speak of balance?
Or is this me searching for something more?
I wake in the morning
And one side always aches
What am I holding onto in this space?
What have I not resolved?
I have happiness
So why does this anxiety still trickle down my spine
And settle in my stomach?
This is my life
NOT YOURS, I scream
MINE!

*Jaclyn Villavicencio*

I'm sorry
But I can no longer lie to you
I can't say you are all the things
That you aren't
To them
They see greatness
To me
I see absence
You weren't there
And there is nothing
I can say
To make you feel better about that
Or to help you navigate your guilt
Figure it out
I had to

*A Heart Full of Lavender*

I think you like
Making the hair on my neck stand up
Every time I think I've rid myself of you
You come breathing down my back
Reminding me some wounds
May never heal

*Jaclyn Villavicencio*

She's back again
This version of me I despise
The short-tempered one
Impatient
Buzzing with anxiety
She traps my throat
Her fingers grip tight
My body is boiling
I can't think straight
If I could run
I'd be gone by now
But she has me choked out
All I can do is hold my breath
And wait for her storm to pass

*A Heart Full of Lavender*

Hear my roar in the morning
When you've crept into my dreams
And turned them into nightmares

You've slipped into my consciousness again
And shattered any chance of light
I had left

You escaped the prison of my thoughts
Where I bury your existence
Deep within me

And no matter how hard I try
Your darkness is relentless
And eats me whole

*Jaclyn Villavicencio*

I'm knocking down the bottles in my cabinet
Searching for a tonic that can purge me of you
Because everywhere I look you're there
Ripping out my insides
Destroying my heart
Twisting my stomach
Scratching at my skin
You are the anxiety in my mind
The paranoia in each of my steps
One more day of this
I'll be ripping out my hair
So I'm searching for a tonic
Pour me up something strong
And purge me of everything
That is you

*A Heart Full of Lavender*

Where do I go from here?
My lips are cracked and dry
From all the blood that dripped out of me
From all the energy I've spent
Trying to keep myself together
Now I've crumbled to the ground
Thirsting for someone to love
For someone to pick me up
And take me to the ocean's edge
Where the waves can crash around me
So I won't be the only one falling
Laughing as the water takes hold of me
And tosses me like a rag doll
If I'm to be out of control
May it be in a place I feel most alive

*Jaclyn Villavicencio*

My roots are fragile
When they bend they break
And most days they are too defensive
To take in any water
But you reap what you sow
And with a little extra care
I know I will grow
And my flowers will bloom
When I am ready

Hold on dear one
Do not give it all away
The soil is calling you home
And it will take everything
Inside of you
To get to where you are going

*Jaclyn Villavicencio*

# Part III
## *Feed the Flowers*

*Jaclyn Villavicencio*

The Earth is starting to bloom again
*Just like you.*

*A Heart Full of Lavender*

She adored you
Like spring flowers admire butterflies
Tilting their heads up in delight
Their flowers take full bloom
As they wait for fine flutters
To dance upon their petals
Knowing they should take it all in
While it lasts
Because just as quick as they come
Is also how fast they fly away
And even though butterflies do tend to
Fly back from time to time
A flower always knows there is no guarantee
And yet they still grow every spring
To wait patiently for the ones they love

*Jaclyn Villavicencio*

It's okay to break
Over and over again
It's okay to drop to your knees
Tear up the dirt
Only to plant new seeds
Because even in the darkest night
The moon still holds a light
For all the spaces
You soon will grow

*A Heart Full of Lavender*

I know you felt it when I walked away
I guess you figured I'd always be your victim
But how the tables turned
When I sucked my teeth into your pulsing neck
And drained you of your worth
Leaving you to fall apart

*We both know karma now*

*Jaclyn Villavicencio*

You placed me in a box
Among stacks of pressed flowers
Hoping you could keep me
Pinned between your pages
But this flower needs to breathe
This flower needs to be set free

    I will not be one of your forsaken treasures
    **For I am my own**

*A Heart Full of Lavender*

Some days what you need is a warm bath
You light candles and dim the lights
And the water comforts your soul

But there may be other days

Where what you need
Is to lay in the dead grass
Staring at the gray sky
Crying out why to anything that will listen

And it may not feel like it now

But one day what you'll need
Is to go back to the place you laid and cried
Just so that you can find
A field of flowers in the same place
You thought you would die

*Jaclyn Villavicencio*

**Sometimes you need the sun**

Sometimes you need the sun
Because things don't always go as planned

Sometimes you need the sun
To remind you that you can create your own paradise

Sometimes you need the sun
To remember what it feels like to have something dancing on your skin

Sometimes you need the sun
To warm all the parts of you that have turned cold

Sometimes you need the sun
To remember what your light looks like

*A Heart Full of Lavender*

Soften your heart
*And let the sunshine in*

*Jaclyn Villavicencio*

There is something about spring flowers
They are the first to bloom
After a long, dark winter
Yearning for the sun
But not scared of the cold
That's *bravery*
Blooming even against the odds
And just because you chose to grow
I know you will make it through

One thing I have learned about life is that you have to be proactive. You can't wait around thinking things are going to be done for you or happen for you or that they will fall into place. Of course, sometimes they do, but oftentimes, it is you that will have to create the life that you want. Your sweat. Your tears. It is you that will have to pick up the phone to call an old friend. It is you that has to wake every day giving it your best shot, with a smile on, and a heart wide open. No one can do it for you and it may take all that you have, but in the end, it will be worth it.

*Jaclyn Villavicencio*

I saw blooms yesterday
And it made me smile
As I realized that even when
Your trees are empty and bare
There is still hope out there

*A Heart Full of Lavender*

    Pull me out of the Earth
        And dangle me by the roots
            And still
                You will watch me grow

*Jaclyn Villavicencio*

Tend to your garden
Open up your blinds
And let the sunshine in
Water your roots
And rest your weary head
The time is coming
For you to **g r o w**

Don't be mad at the rain when it comes. It didn't come to harm you. It came to serve as a gentle reminder that sometimes you have to stay in. Sometimes your heart depends on it. Some days we forget to rest...and then the rain comes. Some days we forget to cry...and then the rain comes. Some days we forget to let go...and then the rain comes. And after the drops settle, the clouds will part ways, and the sun will shine again. You will begin to bloom. You will continue to grow. So, don't be mad at the rain when it comes. When you listen to its messages, you'll see how much you've been waiting for it to arrive.

*Jaclyn Villavicencio*

It is time to trim my branches
And get rid of this dead weight
I can't hold onto your forbidden fruit
It's time to let you go

When you hold onto your story so tight, you may never be able to let go. You may never be able to realize that there is still time to write a new chapter, a new ending. Let go of what has happened to you and open yourself up to all the possibilities yet to come.

*Jaclyn Villavicencio*

In my hand, I held the seeds that made me
I sprinkled them upon the Earth
Pushing them in the dirt with my fingertips
And felt my heart begin to bloom

*A Heart Full of Lavender*

I can hang onto it all
Or I can choose to let it go
Your bad mistakes
Won't weigh heavy on my soul
Any longer

*Jaclyn Villavicencio*

Sometimes I wonder if I will be alright
But then I look into your eyes
And I know I have to make it out alive
Not for me
For you
For a chance at a life not riddled with pain
But created in love
In this life, if I'm remembered for anything
If I do anything right
I hope it is that I made you
And that I raised you

You have to learn to enjoy the moments
As anxiety creeps in
You have to be able to say:
*Look anxiety,*
*I am safe*
*I am secure*
*I am protected*
*I am ready to live*
*And you are no longer welcome here*

You deserve to experience this life
to the fullest capacity
You deserve all the joy
And laughter
And bliss
Our Universe offers
**Remember this.**

## Jaclyn Villavicencio

I know what it feels like to feel like you are nothing. A feeling that you don't necessarily believe, but you've been made to feel that way over and over again. Listen to me when I tell you this: hurt people - hurt people. So, if you are waking up today and choosing yourself, walking in kindness, overcoming the obstacles you've been handed, and the trauma they caused you, then you must know that you are not what others have made you feel. Oh, no, not at all. You are everything beautiful and pure in this world. You are a fighter and you've won this battle and you will continue to win the war that has been waged on you. Whatever you do, do not give up on yourself. We need you.

*A Heart Full of Lavender*

If you do anything today
*Work on your healing*

*Jaclyn Villavicencio*

It is okay to be angry
Until you are screaming at the moon
Asking her why she left you in the dark

She will reply with this:

*Just like you feel the dark now*
*Soon you will feel brand new*
*And hang full in the sky*
*While everyone watches you glow*
*In awe*

*A Heart Full of Lavender*

If you needed to hear that you are a beautiful,
powerful, strong, fierce, badass, warrior woman,
I'll tell you anytime
Because I know it deep within my bones
I know it
So, say the word
And I'll be there
To tell you

*Jaclyn Villavicencio*

I've found a place with clear skies
Where the stars shine so bright
And although I know clouds will come
Sometimes they will come without warning
I know I am right where I need to be
To find my healing

Turn on your favorite song
And D A N C E

*Jaclyn Villavicencio*

Never underestimate
The power of laughter
A jar of wildflowers
A glass of red wine
And taking off your bra
As soon as you walk in the door
If you're looking to heal
**Start there**

## A Heart Full of Lavender

A part of healing is to let go
These words
Scribbled down
Between late nights
Long drives
And coffee sips
Is me letting go
Is me *healing*

*Jaclyn Villavicencio*

Whoever was the first to discover that driving down backroads with the windows down, listening to the saddest love song turned all the way up, and singing with tears running down your cheeks, was the first step to healing

*...I want to hug you.*

*A Heart Full of Lavender*

If you do anything today, I hope you don't hold onto your anger. It will make a beast of you. It will harden all your edges and steal all of your sunshine. Don't hold onto your anger, my friend. It's okay to feel it. I hope you do, but then, I hope you work through it. I hope you dig through it, cry through it, scream through it, flow through it, and then, I hope you know you can let it go. Please let it go.

*Jaclyn Villavicencio*

I've looked evil dead in the eyes
And stood just as firm
You never took me away from myself

*A Heart Full of Lavender*

I'm more than a survivor
I'm a powerful woman
**You couldn't break**

*Jaclyn Villavicencio*

Her fierce persona was a threat
So you tried to tame her flames
But that's the thing about wild women
Like a phoenix,
she will always rise from the ashes
Even fiercer than before

I used my hands as I prayed for you. Every day and every night. I used my hands to hold a pencil as I wrote to you so that you wouldn't be so lonely every single day you were away. I used my hands to hold yours. I was so happy you made it home. I used my hands to rub your back, comfort you, and let you know I had you. I used my hands to hold your head into my shoulder. I was always there when you needed me. I used my hands to shield my face when you threatened me with your rage. I used my hands to push you away and try to run. I used my hands to wipe the tears off my face after you were finished. It was then I realized the warmness I was feeling down my cheek was actually blood. I used my hands to plead for you to forgive me for whatever I had done. I used my hands to clench into fists wanting to fight back, but too scared to stand. I used my hands to roll up my sleeves and pack up the little that I had. I used my hands to drive away from you for the last time. I used my hands to release my terror and relief. I used my hands to unpack my grief and start anew. I used my hands to tell you I was happy and that you had no place in my life. I used my hands to write about you, to release myself from your trauma, and to save someone else. I used my hands to show there is hope, that things will get better, and you can make it through. I used my hands because for the longest time you used yours to keep mine tied behind my back and now *I am free.*

*Jaclyn Villavicencio*

Your view of a lady just isn't me
Because when I think of a lady
I think of wild and free
She doesn't wear her legs clasped tight
But instead sprawls her velvet vines to the floor
She pulls her world wide open
And then turns pain into pleasure
She isn't strung up too tight
Or held up in corsets
Instead, her breasts lay gently
Naturally on her chest
Her hair stays untamed
And her bed stays unmade
Her fingernails find their way through
The maze
That is your body
And straight down your back
Her lips are soft and sweet
She walks barefoot through your daydreams
And naked in your sheets

*A Heart Full of Lavender*

When you see us walking
With our hips and curves
All shapes and sizes
I hope you feel the wrath that is coming
The wrath that you've awakened
Because I am so damn tired
Of living in a world
Where men think they can lay their hands on a woman
That they can humiliate her
Violate her
Men who believe we should live in fear

*Don't you know who pushed you into this world?*

When you see us walking
I hope you know who's coming
Because we remember our power
Our mystifying ways
Our magic

Your legs will shake and quiver
As you drop to your knees
In awe of the goddesses we've become
*The goddesses we've always been*

You woke up today. You are still breathing. Do not ever think that is not something extraordinary in a world where nothing is promised tomorrow. We live in a world where one child draws their last breath while another child is being born. We live in a world where some of us are so deep in the darkness we don't want to be alive. We walk past each other without ever realizing each of us has our own inner struggles, but when you think about it, what a gracious thought to know we all keep pushing on. Do not ever think for a second that you are not a fighter, a survivor, or an amazing being who is worthy of all you desire. Do not ever think seeing the dawn break isn't a blessing. Do not ever think your life doesn't mean something or that you won't be missed when you are gone.

## A Heart Full of Lavender

When I look in the mirror
I see all the women who have stood before me
The women who held babies on their hips
And spit up on their shirt
The women who prayed for escape
With blue around their eyes
The women who braided their hair
Before a long day of work
That paid for the kids
they were raising all on their own
The women who never stopped
Even when the whole world was against them
The women who wiped their tears
And rolled up their sleeves
and vowed to fight on
When I look in the mirror
I see the tears, tough skin, warm hearts, wrinkles,
gray hair, struggles, and most importantly,
I see the **triumphs**
I see me, I see her, I see you

*Jaclyn Villavicencio*

We are not here for your pleasure
For your entertainment
For your needs
We are not here to spend our nights
Down on our knees
We are not here to make you feel
Big and bad
We are not here hoping that
We are the best you ever had
We are not roles to play out
Or slaves in the kitchen
We are not here just to make babies
Or to serve you all your dinner
We are not lower than you
Or submissive to our leaders
We are not weak or dainty
Or sex symbols
We are none of these
Unless of course,
We CHOOSE to be
Unless of course,
We WANT to be

*A Heart Full of Lavender*

You want us your way or no way
You tell us we must grow
All the flowers in your fields
Even when our soil isn't ready
Then you lay us down in your bed of thorns
Whenever you choose
Because if we say no
You cry like the babies you refuse to care for
After you've filled us up
And rung us out to dry
Pointing fingers at righteousness
When we both know this has nothing to do with
The sun in our sky
This is what control looks like
But you can't control a "bitch"
Who is already free
And quite frankly,
**You can't control me**

*Jaclyn Villavicencio*

# Part IV
*Harvest the Petals*

*Jaclyn Villavicencio*

You called to me in the wind today
As I sat beneath the sycamore
You came in strong and sturdy
Leaving nothing untouched
Awakening the leaves, the trees
Every blade of grass
And each hair on my body
You called to me in the wind today
And reminded me of my power

*A Heart Full of Lavender*

Sometimes you just need that escape
That breath of fresh air
That brings you back to yourself
Never forget that
Because your soul will never allow itself to be caged
And when you listen closely to what it whispers
You will hear when it is begging to be freed
Listen
And let yourself go

You can wake up every morning still holding onto the past. The pain, the regret, the memories. You can wake up every morning only looking toward the future. The wants, the expectations, the anxiety, the fear. Or, you can wake up every morning looking into the now. The only promise you really have. The breath, the joy, the laughter, the clouds, the birds outside your window, the music you just turned on, the floor waiting for you to dance upon. This moment that is yours that you can turn into anything you want.

*A Heart Full of Lavender*

Sing to me sweet bird
Every morning I hear
The promise of a new day

*Jaclyn Villavicencio*

We can sit and drown in our self-destruction
Or we can choose to rise into a new day

*A Heart Full of Lavender*

I looked in the mirror today
And said I love you
Just as I do every morning
But today
*I believed it*

*Jaclyn Villavicencio*

I hear her calling me
She's holding out her hand
Placing doves and lilies at my feet
I begin to feel a softness in my heart
Telling me I am finally free

*A Heart Full of Lavender*

You are explosively stunning
I say to the woman in the mirror
I still can't believe she is me

*Jaclyn Villavicencio*

You are a field of flowers
That should dance in the breeze
Never let anyone trample on you with dirty feet
You are meant to grow onwards
Outstretched towards the sun
Basking in your wild
Running in your free
Spreading all your magic out to the sea

*A Heart Full of Lavender*

She came to a point in her life
Where she chose to let it go
This is her wishing you well
It took her a long time to get here
To let go of the anger
The trauma that still sets in
The sadness and the fear
But the gift of hope
Of courage
Of peace
Those were the greatest gifts
She could ever receive
So this is her
Wishing you well

*Jaclyn Villavicencio*

From your pain
A seed will be planted
Deep down in your soul
And once all the water is drained
Lavender will grow

They don't want you wild
Because that is where you find your free
That is where you find your power
That is where you find your love
And once you are there
They can no longer hold you back
They don't want you wild
But I say
**Let down your hair**

*Jaclyn Villavicencio*

Weaving in and out
The wild summer river flows
And returns me home

*A Heart Full of Lavender*

They want to cut you down
To rip you apart
And cut off your source
But that's the thing about peace
Once you find it
It is yours forever

*Jaclyn Villavicencio*

My forgiveness isn't your freedom
**It's mine**

Sometimes people hurt you because they are hurting. They hurt you and they don't even know it. Your choices have ripple effects that circumference more than you may know. Impulse is a bitch. *Choose wisely.*

*Jaclyn Villavicencio*

You wrapped barbed wire
Around my body
And tried to pull tight
To keep me in your cage
And still, you couldn't break me
You just taught me how to fly

*A Heart Full of Lavender*

I am more than what you made me
*I am everything I still believe in*

*Jaclyn Villavicencio*

The thing about forgiving
Is that I can be exactly who I hoped I'd be
Before you came and wrecked my world
I'll be her and so much more

*A Heart Full of Lavender*

I laid upon the fertile soil
And dug my fingertips into the rich ground
She greeted me happily
And wrapped her vines
Around me arms
To hold me close
She sprinkled dried nettle along my torso
And acacia around my heart
A chestnut bud was placed on my forehead
And she braided daisies in my hair
I lay there looking at the
Pink and purple sky
As the sun began to set
And smiled at all her blessings
As she carried me back home to myself

*Jaclyn Villavicencio*

When the time comes to harvest all your pain
I hope you pick the petals
And lay them out to dry
So the sun soaks up all your sadness
And turns it into joy
Then,
I hope you place your petals safely
Against your heart
As a token of your strength
And the peace you have finally found

*A Heart Full of Lavender*

I wish I could write
about rainbows and butterflies
But I once knew a girl
who was too scared to speak
She carried so much weight upon her shoulders
But now she has a voice
And I can't let her be silenced

*Jaclyn Villavicencio*

This is me licking my wounds
*And turning them into gold*

*A Heart Full of Lavender*

Let this be hope
That a new day will come
A day when you
Will feel at ease
Like a field of Lavender
You will find your peace

*Jaclyn Villavicencio*

Our feet were made to point us forward
A reminder to not look back
Our legs were made to stand us up strong
A reminder we are mountains
Our spine was made to keep us straight
A reminder that if we bend too far we will break
Our arms were made to hold us tight
A reminder that our bodies are our home
Our hearts were made to beat in our chest
A reminder we are still alive
Our lungs were made to breathe big and slow
A reminder that we can alter our inner world
Our bodies are so much more than what we've been led to believe
They are our strength, our guide, our comfort, our calm, our healing
*Our home*

*A Heart Full of Lavender*

When it is all said and done
Please take me to the sea
Where I will dance upon your skin
So effortlessly
Let's buy a house where our children can go
Nestled between cottages
In our favorite coastal town
Where we will lay
Entwined in the tall grass
That grows in the sand
Back to the place
Where our hearts first met
And poured out into Earth's waters

*Jaclyn Villavicencio*

You can find me where the waves crash
Along the golden coastline
Salter water gusts of wind
And lavender in my hair

*A Heart Full of Lavender*

Pink carnation petals
*She gave me something to believe in*

*Jaclyn Villavicencio*

There she stood
Her arms wide open
Dripping in carnations
And plumeria petals
Her scent was like a distant memory
That only a child knows
Her smile said *Come in*
And they talked for hours
Nestled on chairs
In the room where she spoke her love language

*A Heart Full of Lavender*

I come from a long line of strong women
On both sides of my family tree
The kind of woman
That creates magic
When she walks through a door
And shatters glass hearts
When she leaves

*Jaclyn Villavicencio*

In my mason jar
I carry lavender petals
I sprinkle them
In my bath
In my tea
I sprinkle them all over me
As a reminder of the peace
I've found
A reminder of the calm
And now I pass them on to you
As a reminder that you are worth it
Even after you've been broken down
And pulled apart
After all you've been through
Just remember
Sometimes it is in the breaking
That you find your healing

*A Heart Full of Lavender*

Today I choose forgiveness
I breathe in my healing
And breathe out my forgiveness to you
May it fill your soul and relieve you of your guilt
So that you may be free from your weight
I just want to see you happy
Finally

*Jaclyn Villavicencio*

I bundled you up like lavender
And held you in close
Knowing this moment
Would one day soon
Be a distant memory

When something good comes around, I hope you are ready. I hope you hold it delicately in your hands and never take it for granted. I hope you mend the soil and nourish the roots. I hope you let it flourish in the golden hour. Make sure you are ready when something good comes around because a moment like that doesn't happen often.

*Jaclyn Villavicencio*

So we meet again
With the floor at my back
And my body stretched open
A glorious feeling
This moment I have found
Curled up in just me
Experiencing this beautiful place
That comes when I breathe

*A Heart Full of Lavender*

I feel seen for the first time in forever
Like every single part of me
Is being kissed by flower petals
Like the clouds have parted way
And the sun is meeting my skin for the first time
It's like a first kiss
When the heat rises in your body
I feel seen for the first time
And it is so special because I feel seen by
Me
Myself
My own heart
And by my own light
And at this point
If no one ever loves me
I frankly don't give a damn
Because I love me
And that is saying something

*Jaclyn Villavicencio*

I never thought I would find my truth
With my knees bent in the dirt
Sweat dripping down my back
And my fingers deep within the soil
Ripping out every last bit of your wolfsbane
That poisoned me

And now that the work is done
I watch for aster and lilac to grow
*redemption

*A Heart Full of Lavender*

My heart is beating out flower petals
That fill up my bloodstream
And relax my soul
I'm floating on a lazy river
A river of love
That is overflowing with peace
May this current never change

*Jaclyn Villavicencio*

My words may not mean a thing to you
But to me
They are the air that I breathe
The blood in my bones
The ache in my chest
Thumping to be freed
They are the ignition to my soul
And the dreams I still believe in

*A Heart Full of Lavender*

One day you will look back
And you won't be able to recognize her
But please remember not to forget her
Even in her darkness
In all her despair
She needs you to remember
So you never forget
What turned her heart cold
And how hard she fought
To feel alive again
The battles she won
For your light to grow
And the nights that still come to haunt her
You owe it to her
To become everything
She dreamed of
But thought would never be possible

*Jaclyn Villavicencio*

Take a deep breath in the morning
Tilt your head up to the sun
Listen to the sounds that greet you
And sing back to the bluebirds
It's okay to feel alive
It's okay to be happy
**You worked so hard for this**

*A Heart Full of Lavender*

I needed you
Like the sunflowers need the sun
I tilted my head up to the sky
And you brought me home

*Jaclyn Villavicencio*

He brings me tea
With extra honey
I love the way he wraps the bag
Around the mug handle
As the tea steeps

                                          I wonder if he even
                                              knows I notice
                                    Or that I would go through
                                         all the heartache
                                                  over again
                                                   *All of it*
                              If it meant that I would end up
                                        right here with him

## A Heart Full of Lavender

It still surprises me
That you picked me
From a garden of pretty blooms
You chose me
A flower with missing petals
And withered leaves
It still surprises me
That you never turned from me
Even when my storms came
You held me even closer
So that I'd be safe
Even when they tried to pull me away
It still surprises me
That you still long
For my hand
Even after it has spent the afternoon
Digging in the dirt
It still surprises me
That you think so much of me
When sometimes I can barely
Look at myself in the mirror
It still surprises me
After all this time
That I haven't ruined you yet

*Jaclyn Villavicencio*

Could it be we saved each other
From all the pain life had thrown our way
Both finding our own way to numb the burn
Until the day we found each other
And our frozen veins melted away
New life pumped through us
Shining light from every corner of our souls
On that day, you were inscribed into my heart
And I into yours
Forever

*A Heart Full of Lavender*

I don't know if I could ever repay you
Or thank you for accepting me
Just the way I am
And loving
Every broken piece

*Jaclyn Villavicencio*

She was just a shell
When he first met her
Skin and bones
Fear placed where muscle
Used to grow
So he took her to the water
To help mold her back together
And pour life back into
Her veins
The salt healed her wounds
The waves pushed out the pain
And as the tides pulled out
They basked in the calm
Together

*A Heart Full of Lavender*

Now I know
I'm honeysuckle
Thick and sweet
I'll take away your pain
I'll make you breathe
Come dance upon my petals
And feed off my nectar drip
I can give you what you want
Sip by sip
This is my power
As I stretch upon the trees
I'm happy now
And happiness is me

*Jaclyn Villavicencio*

I feel alive
Laying here
My back flat to the floor
I can feel my blood
Rushing through my body
My heart pumping
In my chest
I feel good
I am so grateful
I found all my pieces
And carried me back home

*A Heart Full of Lavender*

I've come to a point in my life
Where I have found the most
unconditional love
For myself
I look at her in the mirror
And I am so enamored
So proud
*You made it mama*
*And you keep making it*

Even if you don't believe it now
Look at yourself in the mirror until you do

*Jaclyn Villavicencio*

I guess I had what it took all along
To save me from your wrongdoing
*Myself*

*A Heart Full of Lavender*

I come from hills that roam
On mountain peak tops
And magic spells
Hidden by idols of man
I come from hills that roam
I know who I am

*Jaclyn Villavicencio*

I open my windows
To listen to the songbirds sing
And watch the hill
Of grass
Turn back to green
The world is changing again
Spring has returned
We've made it through the dark days
And opened our blinds to the rising sun
This air,
So clean and bright
Deserves to be taken in
I open my windows
To let out this dust
That has been trailing off my skin
All winter
And I step outside
Amongst the others
Reborn
Renewed
Smiling wide because
We made it through

They say crows feet like it is a bad thing
These wrinkles around my eyes
Are a testament
To all the nights they closed
With tears pouring over
And all the mornings they reopened
Ready to take on another day
Despite it all
I earned these wrinkles
Through all the hurt
The pain
The fear
That turned to
The joy
The happy
The love
They say crows feet like it's a bad thing
But I wear mine proud

*Jaclyn Villavicencio*

And one day she chose
To silence out all the noise
In her head
That told her she would never
Be good enough
And instead
Stepped into the woman
She already was
Who would never let
Anything
Hold her back again

## A Heart Full of Lavender

*Note to self:*

You are still the softness you were born with
The warm heart overflowing with love
You are still the silly spirit
And you still can walk with ease
You are still the calm that came
Before the storm

*Jaclyn Villavicencio*

Sometimes you have to be your own light. Some days come and it will feel like the sun never shines for you and you will have to choose to shine. Some days getting out of bed will be the hardest thing you have ever done, and still, you will have to be the driving force that stirs you from your desolate slumber. Life is not easy, and it never will be, but it can be filled with so much joy and love. More than you may be able to even imagine right now. And some days, you may have to choose to be that joy and that love. There will be times when no one is in your corner, when people are betting on you to fail, and the shadows are your only friend, and still, you will have to choose to be your own light. I am telling you though, that when the dust settles, and the clouds part, you will be so glad you weathered the storm and that your light didn't fade.

*A Heart Full of Lavender*

They say it is hard to grow lavender
And I'd agree that is right
I worked so hard for this peace
I sleep with at night
You see,
I now have a heart full of lavender
After all the heartache that came
And although it wasn't easy
I grew strong roots
To find a way to push through
And make a life I am grateful for
A life surrounded
By bluebirds
Who hold me with love so tight
So I strive every day to find my light
To shine upon the lavender
That I planted in the cold
And took so long for me to grow
The lavender that brought me home

*Jaclyn Villavicencio*

I woke to a field of dandelion and clover
And a soul that has been cleansed of you
These words are my tincture
Amongst an apothecary of pages
That free me from your vile torment
A vial that I used to wear around my neck
But I ripped it off last night
Threw it to the floor
And as the glass cracked
Your power slipped away
I can finally say
*You do nothing to me*

*A Heart Full of Lavender*

Remember that time I thought I'd never get rid of you / Well, now I wear a name tag above my heart that reads *peace* / and when I go dancing in the streets / Lavender falls from my pockets / That sprinkle me with sweet dreams / So when I wake in the morning / I open my eyes to eyes that see me / And hands that feel me just as I am / I have feelings that I'm not scared to feel / While I'm wearing them / I also have a smile and a laugh that I don't mind using / I feel good in my skin even on days when my belly falls over my jeans / I'm fine being me / Because this woman I walk in / Is strong and mighty / She doesn't mind being a fighter / But damn when she's a lover...she's a *lover* / And I love her quick way with words / The way she makes heads turn / She has a determined spirit / That can catch herself when she fucks up / But also can lift herself when she falls / And she's all of these things / Even after you / She battled your storm / And became her own sun / That grew more out of the garden / You trampled on / Then you will ever get to know.

*Jaclyn Villavicencio*

Let's take a moment
A deep breath in
And a breath of love out
For all the women
Who never made it out
Who never made it back home to themselves
We owe it to them
To live a full life of breathtaking peace
Love and beauty
May our tears kiss the earth
And travel to their souls
So they know they are not alone

*A Heart Full of Lavender*

I hope you read these words
And you don't feel sorry
You have a story, too
This just happens to be mine
I hope you read these words
And are inspired to tell your own

*...This is the way to peace.*

*Thank you for reading,*

*Jaclyn*

*About the Author*

Jaclyn Villavicencio is a fierce spirit, and wild soul, with a passion for self-healing and empowering women. A Maryland native and mother of three wild boys, she currently resides with her family where the mountains meet the farm. When she isn't writing poetry, you can usually find her reading something romantic, attempting watercolor, by the ocean, or anywhere her family is. She shares much of her work writing under her pseudonym Crescent Mother on Instagram (@crescent_mother). You can find more of her work and shop her art on her website www.crescentmother.com.

Printed in Great Britain
by Amazon

38168645R00121